Dressed for th

Contents

Northcott School

Written by
Emma Lynch

Many different clothes

helmet

Have you ever noticed that we wear many different kinds of clothes?

face mask

Clothes can protect us and help us
to do our jobs.

Clothes to be noticed

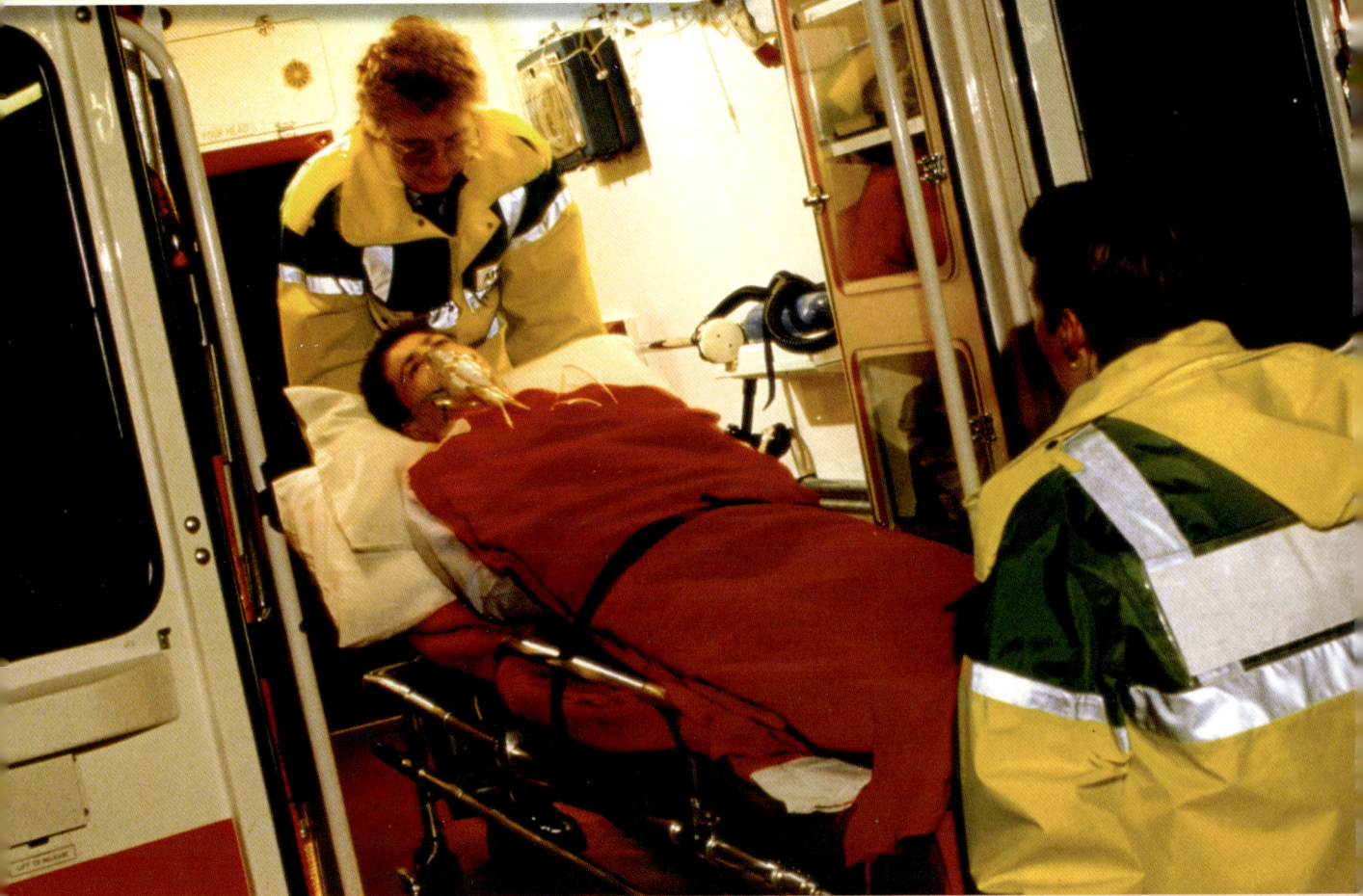

Ambulance drivers wear bright clothes so we can spot them in a crowd. If they race to help at an accident, we let them through.

Cyclists wear shiny strips on their clothes.
Car drivers see the cyclists and keep
their distance.

Clothes for far-out places

Fleecy clothes protect this explorer from the **intense cold**. He wears a whistle so he can call for help in a snowstorm.

Gravity boots
help spacemen
to walk on
the moon.

A spaceman wears a helmet and great
big gravity boots.

Clothes for making a scene

This cinema actor is making a film at the castle. He is dressed for a fight scene.

A circus acrobat needs to have great balance.

Circus acrobats wear fancy costumes. They look very graceful.

Clothes for playing sport

Footballers wear boots with laces at the side. The laces stay out of their way when they kick the ball.

A helmet protects the player's face from the ball.

Cricket players protect their legs from the fast pace of the ball.

Clothes for defence

This scientist wears clothes that hide her body. This is so that **acid** can not get on her skin.

Everyone in the operating room wears a mask.

Doctors and nurses wear gowns over their clothes.

Your clothes

Do you sometimes have to wear different kinds of clothes?

Why do you need to wear these clothes?

Glossary

acid　　　　　　chemical that can burn skin

fleecy　　　　　woolly, like the coat of a sheep

gravity boots　boots that weigh a lot

intense cold　　very cold